Choose hope and love

Louise Alder

BookLeaf Publishing

India | USA | UK

Presentation by *BookLeaf Publishing*

Web: www.bookleafpub.com

E-mail: info@bookleafpub.com

ISBN: 9789358737806

First edition 2023

ACKNOWLEDGEMENT

With all my love and gratitude to my wonderful parents, sister, brother in law, niece, nephew, fantastic bunch of friends and medical team without whom I'd not be the person I am today. They keep me safe, comforted and hopeful. Thank you all from the bottom of my lucky heart x

Cracks let the light shine through

I once heard someone tell me
life's cracks let light shine through
And all along, true friends will help
to fix us back like glue

You're high up in my trusted tribe
so thanks for being you
I trust one day, with help and love
we'll find our 'hiding' Lou

For now, she's in the shadows
as she heals to glow once more
but in between, your words and thoughts
are all she can ask for

In darkest times, the true stars shine
and you do gleam so bright
Thanks for being so damned ace
and turning up the light

You truly make a difference
you cheer me on my way
I hope it won't be long until
we laugh as one each day.

My wonderful neighbours

When I feel so scared and sad
I think of you and fun we've had
I know you love me, know you care
I know you two are always there

I'll do my best to get well soon
Lou's just hiding, next door room
We'll find the key, unlock the door
And we can hug again once more ♥

Hope is a wonderful thing

The tunnel looks so dark, so bleak
each hour ahead drags like a week
You ache with dread, you shake with fright
and all this time, you're blind to light

With strength, with help, with time, with love
Glimmers blink, a power above
You'll start to feel you are still there
you'll see the grass, you'll smell the air

Hope holds so much promise close
This too will pass, forgotten ghost
Dig deep, stay strong, the world needs you
As I fight on, will you please too?

Never ever give up.

Chips

What is life without hot chips?
The kind that make you lick your lips
Salty, crunchy, fluff inside
Tomato sauce completes the ride!

I know a moment on the tongue
leads to fat upon my bum
But for this quick fix, I don't care
I'll just buy bigger jeans to wear!

Jokes aside, they're a rare treat
compared to all the good I eat
I'll aim to burn them off by walking
Not just sitting down and talking

I'm working hard to persuade me
that striding out can help me 'be'
Sat here solo at the pub
I've founded my own writing club

The words are flowing with my drink
My brain has slowed, I'm clear to think
'Find a way that works for you'
That's what I've been told to do

I think this may be my solution
At least for now, it's my conclusion
Steps and words will help me heal
(as well as chips for every meal)!

Best friends

I owe so much to my best friends
They cheer me up with words they send
they've cared for me for months and months
Twists and turns, blips and bumps

I love them loads and they love me
We are a lucky 'family'
They're all the best, I truly feel
Kind, strong and mighty - keep things real

In recent times I've brightened up
I'm pouring from a fuller cup
The clouds are parting, hope's ahead
No more dreaded tears in bed

I hope these girls all realise
how much I really care
appreciate and thank them all
For simply being there x

Good Morning

Please don't take for granted
waking up each day
For some, this privelege is snatched
and stolen without say

Even when you just see dark
and all you feel is dread
You're here; alive and have a chance
to seek some hope instead

Breathe in the air, gaze at that sky
for it'll help your fight
if this is all you do today
know that that's alright

Tomorrow never truly comes
today's the day we hold
baby steps, hour by hour
Stay strong and brave, be bold

Niece & Nephew

Niece and Nephew - what a joy
A feisty girl, a cuddly boy
They bring such sun into our lives
I love to watch them grow and thrive

They bounce like springs on trampolines
Their eyes light up with cold ice creams
Their energy, it knows no bounds
Exploring toy shops
Clutching pounds

'Read to me please Auntie Lou'
'But climb in bed before you do'
My nephew likes to snuggle down
Ending chapters met with frown

'I can dance and I can twirl'
'I can cartwheel, I can whirl'
My niece may be teeny tiny
but her force and strength are shiny!

Life

In this funny thing called life
we're dealt with all sorts; peace and strife
The path is sometimes smooth as glass
at others, it's a bumpy pass

Whichever road you're on right now
keep moving forward; steady, slow
Celebrate a joyful pace
or shuffle by, no need to race

The lane will twist, the track will turn
and that is how we grow and learn
Step by step and bit by bit
will furnish us with strength and grit

If the sun is beaming down
enjoy the warmth and don that crown!
If the clouds are looming dark
have faith one day they'll move apart

I hope today's a happy one
and all of us can find some fun
with strength and hope, with love and kind
Please know you're warmly on my mind.

Fun memories

When I'm flat and feeling blue
I think of good times spent with you
The laughs, the wines, the jokes, the fun
You truly are my source of sun

Rain

The rain falls down like diamonds
and shimmers from the skies
like little gems cascading south
from all the angels eyes

without the rain we'd have no flowers
I try to think like this
instead of moaning 'ugh, how gross'
why not 'this grass looks bliss'!

A day of two halves

If the day starts bad for you
remember it might not end blue
or mood can shift, our mood can change
Believe me, I've seen the full range

Have faith the day could shine with time
Be hopeful you will sleep just fine
This rollercoaster twists and turns
and through the clouds, the sun still burns

Sometimes just one beam of light
will spur us on, we'll be alright
Look out for that single ray
which may well make things feel okay

My tears

As tears drip streaming down my face
It feels so sure they're in a race
Which one will reach my jumper first?
My hopeful bubble promptly burst

I wail, I slouch, I crumble down
The brief worn smile turns into frown
I try and breathe, my body drops
And crying loudly just won't stop

I want to curl up in my bed
Hide my thoughts, comfort my head
Sleeping makes it go away
Until I wake, tears stay at bay

Another day it dawns again
The thoughts and feelings march like men
they trample through my troubled mind
they're neither friendly nor are they kind

My eyes begin to prick again
Familiar tears, not if but when
The endless anguish that this brings
The doom, the gloom and all those things

Getting up and out of bed
Is not as easy as is said
My energy is sapped and low
My mind is tired, my movements slow

But with time, determination
and a lot of courage too
You can get up, you can get dressed
You can find things to do

Be kind to you on days like this
And treat yourself with love
Soothe your body, mind and soul
And search for strength above

For tears won't flow forever
celebrate them gone
This too will pass, your eyes will shine
and then you've truly won!

A smile

Did you know a smile goes miles?
It's universal too!
So why not face the mirror
And beam at lovely you!

For you deserve to feel the joy
A smile or grin is wealth
Don't rely on someone else
You can admire yourself!

Every step

Every single journey
starts with just one plod
So put one foot down, then the next
and get moving that bod!

I know it feels impossible
when you are tired and low
But fresh air, nature, exercise
will fuel your inner glow

A few steps round the garden
is a great way to begin
Get your face up to the sun
and let the goodness in

Believe you me, I know it's hard
I also know it works
to lift your mood, to feel that pride
They're just two of the perks

The devil in your head will say
you can't do this today
prove him wrong and show him up
live your life YOUR way

Gratitude

Each day I try to think
of something good or nice
It doesn't need to be lavish
Or come at a high price

Sometimes it's a cuddle
from a trusted special friend
Other times it's progress
that show I'm on the mend

It could be a nice flower
Or a buzzing bumble bee
How about a tasty meal?
Or a steaming cup of tea

Whatever you decide to choose
gratitude is great
reminds us that it's not all bad
It's not all doom and hate

You are precious

In this big wide world of ours
there's only one of you
So cherish your whole being
and love yourself please too

You're needed, wanted and deserved
you matter oh so much
when things get tough and hard to bear
reach out and get in touch

No man is an island
we all need help in life
So call that friend or dial that line
don't be alone with strife

So please make me one promise
that you'll not suffer alone
there's always someone to talk to
so just pick up the phone

To my family

Sometimes when I lie awake
and think of all the things
I smile about our 'famship'
and all the joy it brings

The gang of us are thick as thieves
I love us all so much
We laugh, we cry, we talk, we hear
we hug, we smile and such

Things aren't always easy
We're sometimes sent a blow
But together we can navigate
along life's path we go

I want you to know just how much
you truly mean to Lou
my heart is never fuller
than in the lounge with you

Thank you to my friends

Guys you are such good friends
Strong and tough, such legends
You listen, care, you're always there
Our fab chats never end

You'll never know how much it means
That you make time for me
You sacrifice, you hug me tight
You make me feel like me

We tell our woes, it ain't all fun
But problems shared are halved
Friends are there through thick and thin
And still we have some laughs

When you think it's been so long
since we met up last time
But like no days have passed us by
You're true true friends of mine

Thanks for everything, my loves
And please reach out to me
A two way street our friendships are
it's not 'me, you' - it's 'we'